The Called

Your Life Predestined

MARY V PATE

Copyright © 2020 by Mary V. Pate
All rights reserved.
ISBN: 13-978057866476-7

This book or parts thereof may not be reproduced in any form, stored in a retrieval file, or transmitted in any form by any means, electronic, mechanical, photocopy, recording, or otherwise, without prior written permission of the publisher and author, except as provided by United States of America copyright law.

Scripture quotations taken from THE AMPLIFIED BIBLE, Copyright © 1954, 1958, 1962. 1964, 1965, 1987
by The Lockman Foundation. All rights reserved.
Used by permission. (www.Lockman.org)

Scripture taken from the New King James Version Copyright © 1982 by Thomas Nelson, Inc.
Used by permission. All rights reserved.

There may be information quoted by the Author from one of her previous books to enhance and provide more knowledge and understanding of that topic.

Cover Page: K&T Graphics
Printed in the USA.
Published by Mary V Pate & Mary Pate Ministries– Laurel Springs, NJ

My frame was not hidden from You, When I was being formed in secret, And intricately and skillfully formed [as if embroidered with many colors] in the depths of the earth.

*-**Psalm 139:15***

Dedication

This book is dedicated to the Holy Spirit for orchestrating my life and giving me the knowledge and wisdom to write His commands. My gratitude is overwhelming because of him. This book will be most valuable to those whom the Holy Spirit has taken your hands and guiding you into his most Holy Place. Your hands are being drawn by Him as He leads you like no other person can. You are not making the decision on your own to step into your *Calling*, it is orchestrated by the Holy Spirit and He alone.

You may be seeking your place in Christian business, your personal life or ministry; and going through hell and high water trying to make the right decisions. Our Father's love is joyous, kind, uncompromising, and eternally fulfilling. You will thank Him for carrying you through excruciating turbulent times and teaching you how to be abased and abound no matter the situations you encounter. He will bring you through the storms, trials, tribulations, tests; and into a life that commands you to teach others about Him (the Holy Spirit) and the importance of building a relationship with Him. Most of all, He will teach you your purpose for being born, so that you can teach others to advance His kingdom. How awesome is that? Enjoy practical steps to guide you through those uncertain times during your journey.

Dedicated to the Holy Spirit

Table of Contents

Introduction 1

Why do You Need this Book? 4

Why did I Write this Book? 6

-1- Mind Your Thoughts 8

-2- Matters of the Heart 14

-3- Why Were You Born? 19

-4- Honoring the Past 24

-5- Humble Leaders 29

-6- Who Are YOU! 32

-7- Self-Sabotage 36

-8- Down but Not Out 40

-9- Setting Boundaries 44

-10- The Invasion 49

-11- Take off the Mask 52

-12- Great Faith 56

-13- Resting in God 62

-14- Discerning the Voice of God 69

-15- Unlock Your Greatness 73

-16- A New Season 76

-17- Licensed vs. Ordained 79

-18- Ordained 81

-19- The Called 85

-20- Conclusion 89

Notes to Myself Pages, for your Personal Notes Included after each Chapter.

Introduction

A few years ago, I did not think I would ever laugh again, but as we continue to live, life does have its rewards. There was a time in my life when I was so broken and messed up. Then, one day I heard a mega preacher state "God is going to make you laugh." I thought to myself, how could this be, but I knew that if I could hold onto God's hand, I would someday laugh again. Why, because I began to trust God. What I did not realize is how long it was going to take before God truly allowed me to laugh again. When I say "Laugh again" I thought of my life being full again, money in my pocket, bills paid on time, living well, going on vacations, just enjoying life. Sixteen years would pass by before these things would begin to materialize in my life again, many days of long suffering.

When you are down and out, it is difficult to explain to another person that you will someday rise again, but I believed it. You see, I knew I was not born to live in poverty. I knew my life was supposed to be so beautiful, because despite everything I was going through, I believed God's promises.

My life was on a downward spiral for many years, and I could not seem to change it. It appears I was caught in a spider web entanglement. I read scriptures, stayed in the presence of God, but nothing seemed to change. Every time I got up, I would fall back down again. I knew God had another plan for my life. Then, one day, I fell on my knees and asked God "Why am I going through this?" My answer basically went along with everything God was doing in my life as He prepared me for my journey with Him.

There may be many times when you will probably compare yourself to **Job,** but God will continue to bring you into a life of humbleness. Like **Job,** be steadfast in the word of God, his grace towards you, and know that no matter what you may go through, the most important thing is to pass the test. I believe that at this point, you realize a few things.

1. Is there anything for you to return too?

2. Who can assist you with what you are going through better than God?

3. Do you have other options?

```
┌─────────────────────────────────────┐
│                                     │
│                                     │
│                                     │
└─────────────────────────────────────┘
```

    When you resolve these answers, you will realize, there are no other options.

    During those years I had several mixed feelings and emotions, changes in life that one will go through when God is taking you on His journey, and you are in your wilderness experience. There are words of knowledge and wisdom to help you through those horrific times.

> *In the day of prosperity be joyful, But in the day of adversity consider that God has made the one as well as the other, So that man will not find out anything that will be after him.*
>   **-Ecclesiastes 7:14**

Why do You Need this Book?

Having this book will teach you how to keep your sanity while the Lord is bringing you into your Christian business, ministry, or your personal life. While I was being brought into ministry, I leaned and depended on the Lord, but I did not have a physical human being I could talk to about my thoughts, what was going on with me, and where I was going. I was literally isolated during these seasons, and the time frame lasted for many years. There were many times when I wished there was someone I could talk too. There are times when you may begin to not trust anyone; it can be an exceedingly difficult period in your life.

Keep this book on your coffee table or nightstand to remind you where you can seek help immediately at times when you may be going through. By no means am I trying to replace the Lord. During those seasons when God is molding, shaping, and teaching you who you will become, for Him; there will be lonely times, persecutions, trust issues, back stabbings, anger and perhaps a lot of pain. The Holy Spirit will always be there for you, but at times, He may seem so far away; even to the point of not hearing and answering you. Trust me, He has not left you.

This journey is like nothing you may have experienced before; but nonetheless, it is part of your ordination by God to bring you into your purpose and destiny. Embrace the ups and downs, but in all give thanks because your future knowledge and ways of life is so much bigger than you are.

"Life is a Journey, Enjoy it!"
- Mary V Pate

Why did I Write this Book?

      The Holy Spirit led me to write this book for all who may need the kind of help that was not afforded to me while going through this process. And as you are reading, perhaps you may know others that need more clarity while they are going through. Share with others to bring them into their walk as well and give them more understanding. This is serious stuff and God wants us to share the knowledge that He gives us. You may already be on your journey or just beginning, but nonetheless; these topics will be fulfilling throughout your lifetime.

      The following topics are major areas where I felt a need for sincere help, but did not get it from a human being, although pain was inflicted by others around me. You see, God had me in a place of learning to walk in **"All Truth."** **"All Truth"** is not an easy place to walk into. Isolation becomes a major factor during these times. Hopefully, this book will take some of the pressure off as you begin to build the life God has planned for you. It is important that we know and understand what God is doing in our lives; however, if the Holy Spirit is the one who is leading your life, know that understanding Him at times will be complicated. However, He will show you the way if you remain teachable.

Remember, this is a journey that will one day bring you full circle into your walk; thereafter, you will begin the great work you are assigned to do for His kingdom.

"All things hold true from God."
- Mary V Pate

-1-
Mind Your Thoughts

The Power of our Thoughts begins in the mind. Therefore, we may hear two voices at times but decide which voice you will command to be the authority of your life. Satan's voice comes to steal, kill, and destroy. His thoughts can become strongholds in your mind if you allow him. Jesus' voice comes that you may have life ever after, and to live abundantly. Once you have made the decision to turn your mind over to Jesus, the work begins.

There are many strongholds, and the mind is the entry way to all strongholds that can form. Take lies for instance; if they become believable, and carried through, now they become strongholds. How, because lies affect how you feel, and what you think? A seed was planted in your mind, and now affecting your emotions, your peace, knowledge, and your daily mindset. If the devil can convince you that your destiny is predetermined by him, then whatever God has planned for your life will not manifest. So, you must turn away from the devil so that God can manifest through your thoughts.

Jesus came so that we may have life, and when you listen and can distinguish His voice from the devil, success is inevitable. You must stay in the word of God and meditate on the scriptures so that understanding, and the fruit of the spirit can manifest in your life.

What is the "Fruit of the Spirit?"

"But the fruit of the Spirit is love, joy, peace, longsuffering, kindness, goodness, faithfulness, gentleness, self-control. Against such there is no law."

- Galatians 5:22-23

Once you begin to understand and hear the voice of the Lord, your life will be so much better. Your thoughts will be focused on the positive things in life, instead of the negative.

Remember, your thoughts command how you feel, how you see things that are going on in your life; and how you view yourself. It behooves all of us to get our thought processes in order. The enemy will continually remind us of our past and our failures, and at times he may try to convince many people to commit suicide. He will use you to do all the wrong things in life, and then laugh at you. Satan is not omnipresent, as God is; therefore, he sends his imps out to do his dirty work. That is, to have you do everything against the will of God for your life.

God will do everything in opposition to the enemy. He came that we might have life, and to live abundantly.

As a people, we must make choices that will sustain our lives for the rest of our lives. God is the way. Keeping our thoughts in order and washed in the blood of Jesus maintains us on a level playing field. Our thoughts become joyous, and open to new and loving relationships, having more peace in our lives, moving forward in the presence of the Lord. It is imperative that you become open minded to walk into your ministry calling, business opportunities and personally so that you will receive all God has for you. Keep your mind stayed on Him and He will direct your path.

When we speak about a thing, we need to be cognizant of what we are saying and why we are saying those words. It is so especially important that we learn to speak what is the acceptable thing to say and do unto God. Out of our hearts come the issues of our lives. For those of you who are still in the childbearing years, you want your children to grow up wholesome and full of the things of God. Therefore, for the most part you are responsible for what your children hear, see, learn, and do. If you start with your children when they are incredibly young, they will not forget in their later years. Our minds, hearts, spirit, and thoughts all work in conjunction with one another; therefore, it is particularly important to understand the things we allow to infiltrate into all four areas of our lives and our children. The bible speaks about these issues:

For the word of God is living and powerful, and sharper than any two-edged sword, piercing even to the division of soul and spirit, and of joints and marrow, and is a discerner of the thoughts and intents of the heart.
― ***Hebrews 4:12***

What voice have you decided to listen to and Why?

Do you think you will gain anything from listening to that voice? Explain.

There is nothing wrong with conversating with yourself and the Holy Spirit especially when you are seeking answers that will fulfill Your lifetime. Be brave, this is a time that will eventually bring forth some of the most challenging and fulfilling times in your life.

> *"Listening to the voice of God will bring you into His joyous peace.*
> *- Mary V Pate*

-2-
Matters of the Heart

Out of the heart comes the issues of life. How often have we heard that message? However, it is so true. When we are coming into ministry, walking into our Christian life, we may feel that there is something so terrible we have done wrong in our past that may be unforgivable by the Lord. Rest assured, there is nothing you or I have ever done that God is not willing to forgive. Since Yahweh forgives murderers, I am sure He forgives you as well. People live and do not forgive, but your Abba Father forgives and forgets. We know that people do not forget your past life, the devil does not forget your past; and they both will remind you of it in an inopportune time. If you have taken your heart to the Lord, and asked for forgiveness of your sins, then it is done. No more questions asked. Let them live in your past, you are on a mission.

You have an important job to do for the Lord; therefore, cleansing you of all unclean spirits is of the utmost importance. First, you must see yourself as a new creature in Christ; to think otherwise is detrimental to your well-being. You are loved by the lord, and if you have any doubts about who you are, read the Word of God. He assures us through several books in the "word" how much he genuinely loves us.

Jesus died for our sins, and you should begin seeing yourself as washed by the shed blood of Jesus Christ. There is always going to be a continuous cleansing that we all will go through to stay aligned with God, but you have got to believe that you are healed in the name of Jesus, and you do not need to carry old baggage everywhere you go.

Be honest with yourself about yourself. Give the control of your soul over to the Holy Spirit and allow Him to cleanse you of all your impurities. Be patient with yourself, write down everything about **YOU** that you do not like and/or would like to change. When we write things down, they become visual to us. After writing them down, pray over them and ask God to remove you of all the things listed and change you into who He wants you to be. The Holy Spirit now begins to work on your behalf. However, be careful, if you are not sure you want your life to be changed in ways that you cannot imagine; do not ask God to change you into the person He wants you to be. I am telling you this because at that moment you probably have no idea what God has planned for your life; and you do not know how He is going to make all the changes, and the length of time it is going to take. I will say, hold on tight, because you are going on a serious journey.

The blood of Jesus paid for our sins. Therefore, you must go boldly before the Lord and ask Him for what your heart desires. Forgiving ourselves is in direct relationship to loving ourselves. When we do not love ourselves, we miss out on the great mercies of God. The Holy Spirit is waiting to make an inroad into your life, and He cannot do that unless you release yourself from your old ways.

Begin seeing yourself as a new creature in Christ. If you have repented for your sins, and asked God for forgiveness, then why not forgive yourself. The moment you ask God for forgiveness and repent, you receive it, immediately. Anything you did in the past has now been relinquished from your life; so, grab hold of the new you and move forward. See yourself as that new vibrant, energetic son or daughter of God. Secondly, forgiving others is particularly important whether they know it or not. Many times, people become offended, and you may not know if you were the one to do so. We must forgive others even if they do not acknowledge the things they have done against you. **Forgiveness is for you.**

I dare not hold grudges against anyone for all the things that have been done against me, said to me, although they may have been unkind. I would be a complete mess if that was the case. I have a statement that I always say to myself in those cases, **"I'm not wearing that."** Simply put, it means that just because someone feels some type of way about me or says unkind words to me does not mean their unkindness is true. Many times, we need to weigh the relevance of what a person is saying about you, rather than reacting to negative behaviors. How you feel and think about yourself as a person determines how you will respond to certain accusations. Usually the person (s) speaking unkindly are the ones who are truly in pain.

> *"Laughing again is a must in our lives."*
> *- Mary V Pate*

Write down the things you would like God to change about you?

Keep a road map of the time frame when you notice change: Example: 1 Month, 3 Months, 6 Months, 1 year or longer.

Notes to Myself

" The Freedom to know who you are is
the new person You will become."
- *Mary V Pate*

-3-
Why Were You Born?

While God was bringing me into ministry; I asked him, **"Why Was I Born?"** Ironically, it took seven (7) years for Him to answer me. I believe the Father wanted me to experience and perhaps execute some of my ministry exercises and realize that I had taken on a new way of life, for Him. He answered me after I had given a women's conference. Later that evening as I was sitting at home and reminiscing about the day, He gave me a visual snapshot of myself while I was standing in the pulpit teaching about the subject of the conference. At that moment, He spoke to me and said, **"That is why you were born."** As always, I become absolutely elated when God shows me something. I instantly went into a time of worship with so much gratitude for Him because I remembered so many years prior that I had asked the question, **"Why Was I Born?"** Seven years later, I received my answer **"Teaching & Preaching the Word of GOD"**. There are no questions that you cannot ask the Holy Spirit. He will always answer at some point in time. Be open to receive.

"

We should want Yahweh to be

pleased with everything we do."
-Mary V. Pate

No matter the circumstances from which you came into this world, there is a reason why you were born. In the beginning, God is the only one who truly knows the answer.

Do you have any idea why you were born?

Have you asked God for the Answer? Explain....

"Your eyes saw my substance, being yet unformed, And in Your book they all were written, The days fashioned for me, When as yet there were none of them."
-Psalm 139:16

This scripture is so awesome. *"Your eyes saw my substance, being yet unformed."* Meaning God saw you and obviously knew you before you were even formed. Believe and receive this in the second portion of the scripture. *"And in Your book, they all were written, The days fashioned for me, When as yet there were none of them…*

Again, the Word is stating that in His book the days of your life had already been written (fashioned-scripted) by Him, when yet there were none of them (**your days did not exist**) and He had you all planned out. Therefore, your life was already preordained by God, situations and circumstances were already set by God, your trials, tribulations and tests, your ups and downs, your ins and outs, your wilderness days, your latter days were already written, before you were born. Lord have mercy! This is a lot to embrace.

How awesome is that? When I begin to dissect this scripture, and retained more and more revelation about it, I didn't want to do anything but praise and worship God for all He had planned for my life, before I was born……Go on, start to praise Him right now no matter where you are….You are alive, and while you are alive, changes should be made, and there are things you must do for God…..You need to be **GRATEFUL!**

I realized this as well while meditating on this scripture. The word says that God knew you before you entered your mother's womb. Since that is the case, then God already knew who your biological father and mother was going to be regardless of the circumstances. Sincerely, I believe so. So, people of God, take heed to the message that God has a plan for your life, loves you like no other human can, and looking forward to you walking in His will and His way.

All I can say is, "you must be very special to God knowing that He would think enough of you, write about you in His Lambs book, fashion your life, and your mother and father didn't know anything about you at that time." Once you understand why you were born, you will be able to move forward in your calling by God.

Shout Hallelujah!

Notes to Myself

It's a great day to be among the living.
- *Mary V Pate*

-4-
Honoring the Past

All ministries are not in the pulpit. There are many areas working in ministry, as layman walking in the will and way of God, assisting the needy in various ways. For example, ministry is your business, working a soup kitchen, leading marches that will lead people in the community for equal rights and justice; and so much more.

When we think of the past, we cannot help but think of people like Dr. Martin Luther King Jr. At an incredible young age, it was shown in many of Dr King's documentaries, that he wanted to be a pastor of a small church. He was not called to pastor inside the church. He was called as an Apostle, and to orchestrate the civil rights movement. This is also why he was born. We must know that God knew he was going to die as a young man. God knows everything. Since He knows us before we enter our mother's womb, you can believe that He knows when you and I will leave this earth forever. However, we do not know what more would have materialized if he had lived.

Martin Luther King Jr. was like a Moses, leading the people through the wilderness out of Egypt. He led the marches in Selma, Alabama, in Washington, despite being spat on, beaten, put into jail, and the numerous threats on his life and his family's lives to the very end. He heard from God and knew that his time was coming to an end. But he did it anyway. Thank God for the many people who marched, lived, and died along the way with him, but it was his ministry. He was like Harriett Tubman, still setting the captives free. Let us not forget that the civil rights movement was for all people.

Although Miss Harriett lived an old age, the records show that she led more than 3,000 slaves out of captivity in the south during slavery times. This was a phenomenal responsibility for a woman and considering the conditions and circumstances that she and others had to encounter during those times. But she heard the voice of the Lord speak to her many times, giving her directions to take the "Black" people and run for freedom. She obeyed the voice of the Lord as He spoke to her and guided her in the way which she should go. She was obedient.

They called her "Moses" as she followed in the footsteps of Moses in biblical times as he led the Israelites out of captivity from Egypt. And we all know what Moses had to deal with, a stiff neck people that only wanted to do what they wanted to do which took more than 40 years to get them to the promised land.

I look at those brave souls that heard and listened to the voice of the Lord, and what is more they "**OBEYED**."

They did not have those should have, could have, would have syndromes. This is not to say that they were not fearful at some point in time, or hesitant in what their responsibilities were. Despite everything, they marched on doing the will of the Lord. When Moses started out, he questioned God several times about his concern of who was going to travel with him. God reiterated to Moses that His presence would go with him. This was God's reassurance advising Moses to not be afraid and that He would be with him no matter what he encountered. Notice in the following scriptures how unsettled Moses was about taking this trip and the many times he questioned God's assurance.

"Now therefore, I pray you, if I have found favor in Your sight, let me know Your ways so that I may know You [becoming more deeply and intimately acquainted with You, recognizing, and understanding Your ways more clearly] and that I may find grace and favor in Your sight. And consider also, that this nation is Your people." [14] And the LORD said, "My presence shall go with you, and I will give you rest [by bringing you and the people into the promised land]." [15] And Moses said to Him, "If Your presence does not go [with me], do not lead us up from here. [16] For how then can it be known that Your people and I have found favor in Your sight? Is it not by Your going with us, so that we are distinguished, Your people and I, from all the [other] people on the face of the earth?"

¹⁷ The LORD said to Moses, "I will also do this thing that you have asked; for you have found favor (lovingkindness, mercy) in My sight and I have known you [personally] by name." ¹⁸ Then Moses said, "Please, show me Your glory!" ¹⁹ And God said, "I will make all My goodness pass before you, and I will proclaim the Name of the LORD before you; for I will be gracious to whom I will be gracious, and will show compassion (lovingkindness) on whom I will show compassion."
Exodus 33:13-19

So, Samuel said: "Has the Lord as great delight in burnt offerings and sacrifices, As in obeying the voice of the Lord? Behold, to obey is better than sacrifice, And to heed than the fat of rams."
-1 Samuel 15:22

Notes to Myself

Victory is yours, walk in it.
- *Mary V Pate*

-5-
Humble Leaders

Take a look at some of the leaders in the Old Testament who heard God's voice and lived out their purpose. Through struggles, hardships, procrastination, interacting with stiff necked people, battles in their own minds, tempted by the devil, wanting to give up on their purpose and destiny; but they continued to walk in God's will and His way.

Abraham – Abram ("The Father [or God] Is Exalted"), who is later named **Abraham** ("The Father of Many Nations"), a native of Ur in Mesopotamia, is called by God (Yahweh) to leave his own country and people and journey to an undesignated land, where he will become the founder of a new nation. His story is found in the Book of Genesis.

Moses – best known from the story in the **biblical Book of Exodus** and Quran as the lawgiver who met God face-to-face on Mount Sinai to receive the Ten Commandments after leading his people, the Hebrews, out of bondage in Egypt and to the "promised land" of Canaan.

David - Described in the Hebrew **Bible** as the third king of the United Monarchy of Israel and Judah, after Miphiboseth. In the **biblical** narrative, **David** is a young shepherd who gains fame first as a musician and later by killing the enemy champion Goliath. In the King James Bible, there are 929 passages that speak of David in the scriptures.

Joseph - In the **biblical** narrative, **Joseph** was sold into slavery by his jealous brothers, and rose to become vizier, the second most powerful man in Egypt next to Pharaoh, where his presence and office caused Israel to leave Canaan and settle in Egypt. His **story** is told in the book of **Genesis 37-50**.

Jesus - In Christianity, **Jesus** is believed to be the Son of God and the second Person of the Holy Trinity. Christians believe that through his crucifixion and subsequent resurrection, God offered humans salvation and eternal life. Most of **Jesus's** life is told through the four Gospels of the New Testament **Bible**, known as the Canonical gospels, written by **Matthew, Mark, Luke and John**. ... **Jesus** was born circa 6 B.C.

We should remember that as Leaders we affect other people's lives. As a matter of fact, our destinies are about the lives of others, not necessarily about us. To benefit others and always glorify God.

Notes to Myself

*"Your journey is your Life; embrace
it as though it belongs to you."*
-Mary V Pate

-6-
Who Are YOU!

OK, now the proof is there. The word states God had everything all prepared for us individually. What happened during the years as you were coming into adulthood, and even after making this great day?

Answers: Life happened, so Who are YOU NOW?
- What changes have you gone through during these years?
- Are you willing to take a stand and make changes, or be pressed until the end?
- Do you take ownership for who you are now?

If you are not in your "happy place", begin to press forward to make your latter days greater. There's work that must be done. First, if you do not know who you are, continue to seek God about it. Secondly, be true to yourself. We have all heard this before, but now is the time to put this to action. Begin to put your dreams back into order again. When we were younger, we had dreams. Well, that should not have changed for today. Begin to see yourself in another place or another time, doing things that perhaps you have not done before. Perhaps it is time to be adventurous. You must know your strengths and weaknesses. If not, you will learn them along the way.

How do you take ownership of who you are? Being truthful with yourself, face your fears, and step out on faith. You may have been through some terrible situations in your life; however, you are still here, and that means something. Life has a way of making you fall, and then allowing you to pick up again. The level in which you make the decision to stay up or down depends on you. It takes time, effort, and patience with yourself, perseverance, and the love of yourself to pick up and move forward.

If you have not moved forward, and something has been holding you back, you must determine what is standing in your way from making changes, no matter your age bracket. Could some of the things holding you back include procrastination, fear, feelings of low self-worth, financial barriers, being in denial, bitterness, or anger? There can be a host of obstacles standing in your way, but no matter the circumstance or situation, your life can change for the better. Once you begin to make changes, start with small steps, and then increase as you move forward. Make your Obstacles become Opportunities.

It is sad to see some people trying to portray others, particularly in ministry. Example, a ministry leader raising up other ministers in church and those ministers want to sound like, be like their leader. Another instance is people in ministry wanting and claiming gifts they do not carry. God is not pleased with this. How will you ever know who you are if you do not seek God about "You." I am absolutely convinced that everyone should seek God about their lives. Ministry should not be about form and fashion, but to teach others about Jesus Christ and live your life walking in love for others.

> *"For I the Lord your God keep hold of your right hand; [I am the Lord], Who says to you, 'Do not fear, I will help you.'*
> ***-Isaiah 41:13***

Notes to Myself

*The quality of your life is not determined
by the quantity of your stuff.*
-Mary V Pate

-7-
Self-Sabotage

One of the major strongholds in people's lives is Self-Sabotage. If you or someone you know is in a self-sabotaging state of mine believe me there is so much time and energy that is wasted doing absolutely nothing. People that sabotage themselves can travel through time from one year to the next and see absolutely nothing change in their lives. A self-sabotage state of mine tells you that if you do not make changes in your life, then you do not have to worry about being embarrassed about your mistakes; you do not have to worry about failing when a task does not work or starting over again. In other words, self-sabotage wants to keep you in a dead-end safe mode.

Do not become confused with being in the wilderness when God is in control. That is a different story, because God will have us going through the wilderness, and we think nothing is changing, but there is change being manifested. We are being changed into the person He wants us to be, changing from the old to the new. Transformation is taking place.

Self-Sabotage involves procrastination, a fearful state of mind, feelings of low self-esteem, a lack of planning, making excuses for not moving beyond your comfort zone, being intimidated by other people's accomplishments, and so much more. This list could go on and on.

However, here are a few steps to eliminate self-sabotage:

- Begin to change your mind set, think positive,
- Set realistic, measurable goals, behavior patterns should change, build your self-esteem, take control of your life.
- Seek professional help or coaching if necessary.

Move beyond the **FEAR** factor, begin to walk in **FAITH**.

The word of God states that we must transform and renew our minds; therefore, it is imperative to do this to change our self-sabotaging mind sets. You want to get to the point of making your life happy, filled with joy, laughing again, and thinking more positively about yourself. Incorporate a new mind set.

> "Therefore, we do not become discouraged (spiritless, disappointed, or afraid]. Though our outer self is [progressively] wasting away, yet our inner self is being [progressively] renewed day by day. For our momentary, light distress [this passing trouble] is producing

for us, an eternal weight of glory [a fullness] beyond all measure [surpassing all comparisons, a transcendent splendor and an endless blessedness]!"
-2 Corinthians 4:16-17

Self-Sabotage sounds like a nasty phrase; and it is if you do not decide to do something about it. If you keep your eyes focused on God, changes will come in your life; all for the glory of God. You will be empowered to move forward in your life and complete the things that you were born to do.

Notes to Myself

"Your journey is your Life; embrace it as though it belongs to you."
-Mary V Pate

-8-
Down but Not Out

Think about the days when you did not have a clue who you were, and no knowledge of where you were going. You can thank God that you have come to a place in Yahweh that leads you to a new awareness of yourself. You have arrived in a place of knowing who really takes care of you while you are "**Down but not Out**."

This is a wonderful place to be, because despite everything you are going through or have gone through, God will always be there with you. This journey, "The Call" is painful to say the least, but it is doable. You have got to want this change that is about to manifest itself in your life so badly that you can almost taste it. Know that everyone God is bringing into ministry or to walk in His will and His way is not going to always go through the same situations, but you will go through some type of pain. Jesus had to endure unbelievable pain; therefore, it is imperative that we learn to beat the enemy through the type of pain we also must endure. That pain is so important because it takes you from your old self to your new self. No pain, no gain.

Continue to walk the beaten path to your destiny, and watch God do miraculous things in your life. He will amaze you at times when you least expect it. Although there may be a time span between when God begins to bring you into your time, and when He may bring you out to begin walking in your season. Do not become discouraged or confused about the timing. Timing is everything with God. I have learned not to lean on my own understanding as well as my own timing. Yahweh has perfect timing. Doors will open, doors will close, you will meet new people, some will go, and some will stay, but life begins to get better. Your walk with Him should be so much lighter as you beigin to see how He moves through your life.

Do not allow the feelings of being **"Down and Out"** leave you in a mindset of "I'm lost, and I don't know what to do." The Holy Spirit is just a call away. Call on Him, cry out to Him and give Him the 411 on what is going on with you. He already knows, but He wants you to acknowledge it as well. It is part of your growth period.

Although you may be struggling at times, stay focused. People, places, and things you encounter during this journey is crucial to your destiny. This is a learning process that God may have you in during this period. You will meet people that are unkind, some that may want to use your gifts for their own purpose, and some that do not want you to know your gifts. Be steadfast and encouraged and all will be well with you. Do not make hasty decisions, judgment calls, or move to swiftly. Pay attention to everything going on around you. This is a time to ask for more "Discernment" in your life from the Lord. You will need it.

> *"He who keeps his command will experience nothing harmful. And a wise man's heart discerns both time and judgment."*
> *-Ecclesiastes 8:5*

Notes to Myself

Make Yourself a Priority.
-Mary V Pate

-9-
Setting Boundaries

Have you set boundaries for your life? Boundaries are the lines you need to keep the people and obstacles out of your life that will have a negative effect on you. Boundaries help us to determine the positive things we should allow into our space as well. We all need boundaries; and while we do have them, set them, and keep those boundaries to have your life move forward to be satisfactory for you. Stay focused on who you are. Be accepting for yourself. Know your likes and dislikes and be prepared to stand and exercise those rights if you must.

It is also important to know your tolerance level particularly in terms of dealing with others while they may be occupying your space. This is important when you are in the company of someone for a short or long period of time, but you may not like their characteristics, demeanor, or the verbiage they speak. You need to know what you allow to occupy your space for any length of time, and how you deal with them matters a great deal.

While setting and keeping the boundaries you have created, you must accept who you are for a time and season. If for some reason, you do not like who you are, and how you respond to others, begin to change your behavior and attitude. Being focused is so important for you to get the results you need and are seeking.

When God has you in a holding pattern; that is to say, when He is orchestrating your steps from point A to point B, there are going to be a multitude of changes, emotional uncertainties, tearing down and building up behaviors, learning processes that will strengthen your character, meeting people who are supposed to be in your life for a limited time only. These people are sent to you or you sent to them for reasons that you may or may not understand in the beginning. No matter what you go through with those people and the circumstances that will arise, they are there for the expansion of your future, and for the purpose and plans God has for your life and theirs.

Some people will be sent along the way to distract you from the will of God, to block your blessings, and to use you for their own good. You may experience feelings of loneliness, abandonment, rejection, feeling out of place, unfriendliness, being misunderstood, jealousy from others, and so much more. Make no mistake about it, God will send the Holy Spirit to comfort you during your down time, and He will keep you grounded to walk in His will and His way. It is at these times when He is now setting boundaries around you to keep you safe and out of harm's way. Those boundaries will protect you from the enemy and He will put a hedge of protection around you that no one can cross. Although, the enemy may try, you are surrounded by your angels with open arms, keeping you lifted when you become weak. By the way, you will become weak at times. I remember at times feeling like all my strength had completely left my body, and I wanted to just cave in. It took some time for me to realize that I was under the wings of the Lord, and my angels were there to protect me, **MERCY – MERCY - MERCY!!**

Evilness becomes "good" when you are walking with the Lord. In time, you will realize that no matter what you went through, it was for your own good. Remember God will allow you to walk in adversity but will take care of you at the same time. He is not going to allow anything to harm you in any way. Taking that much needed break to become revived is absolutely important for your next move. Remember:

> *"And though the Lord gives you the bread of adversity and the water of affliction, Yet, your teachers will not be moved into a corner anymore, but your eyes shall see your teachers. Your ears shall hear a word behind you saying, "This is the way, walk in it, whenever you turn to the right hand, Or whenever you turn to the left."*
> *-**Isaiah 30:20***

"You have set a boundary that they may not pass over, that They may not return to cover the earth."

-Psalm 104:9

Notes to Myself

Do not look back, you are almost there.
-Mary V Pate

-10-
The Invasion

During the time when God is engulfing your life you may often feel like your spirit is being invaded. This usually happens when you are being stripped of some things, and feelings of low self-worth, and confusion may occur. You must remember that there may have been times when you felt in control of your situations and circumstances; however, when God is shaking things up, your life is no longer your own. Being in self-control of your situations are over. You are in a new season, a new period in your life, and God has taken control.

While in this process, the Lord allows you to experience so many different types of emotions; it is amazing. Some of those topics were discussed in previous chapters. But I believe I have mastered this to some degree. When God has a plan and purpose for your life, He already knows that you will meet different people with all types of personalities, and you will probably at some point minister to some of them. Therefore, if you experience those feelings through your own personal life, then you will know how to minister to others.

The love of God is an awesome thing in that He will allow you to be in many types of situations, but He will begin to move you in various ways that will enhance your ability to become the person He wants you to be. Those feelings or invasions are brought forth to build your character. They will make you see life more differently than you ever did before. Embrace those moments as they will take you to another place and level in Him for your life.

Do not allow others to interfere in your flow with the Holy Spirit. He is there to guide and protect you through everything you are going through. Use Him as often as you need to. There is nothing in the world like having that relationship with the Holy Spirit. It is not easy, but if you hang in there, you will begin to get some relief.

I remember when the Holy Spirit was guiding me into ministry, and there were times when I thought I was going to lose my mind; however, the ability to realize that your life is no longer your own makes a world of difference. Take those times profoundly serious as they will eventually assist you when you begin to walk into your destiny.

*"The freedom to know who you are
is the new person you will become."
-Mary V Pate*

Notes to Myself

"Step outside of the Invasion and keep moving."
-Mary V Pate

-11-
Take off the Mask

Yes, it's time to take off the Mask. Your exterior seems OK while your inner being may be screaming for help on the inside.

Typical feelings while wearing the MASK are feelings of shame, guilt, low self-esteem, anger, and resentment, just to name a few. Some may feel a sense of lifelessness, not confident in who they are, and who they would like to become. All the while smiling from the outside and feeling lifeless on the inside, hoping no one knows what is truly going on with them. So, you continue to wear the Mask.

There are so many reasons why people seem as though they're OK but all you need to do is hit their hot spot and they may explode. We have all gone through some type of life issues, it's a part of life. However, answering your Call may be even more excruciating. I remember those days very well. Sometimes, I felt lifeless with so many questions unanswered. Uncertainty became monumental in my life, such as; where was I going, what was I doing, where do I belong, why is this happening to me are just some of the questions that was an everyday event in my life. You see, I didn't understand the process I was going through, and no one to talk with about my issues. I was at a great loss and many disadvantages occurring in my life. I often felt like giving up, but I was determined to live. There were times when things went from bad to worse. What a nightmare that was. I pleaded with God to help me and although He was doing that, I didn't really realize it. I only knew that I was miserable in ways I had never been before. So, when it came time for my total submission to God, I gave in and never looked back. God is on the main line and no matter what you may go through, it's going to be OK. Sometimes very painful, but in the end, God's will be done.

Accepting your purpose and destiny is not always easy but there are things you must do to get yourself in the proper place to hear and receive from God. Avoid people, places, and things that are not going to add any real value to your life. Not in a sense of disrespect, but some people will come into your space to just fill up the space. They will get in the way, distractions of all kinds, and do not want you to go anywhere. These are the ones to avoid. Clarity is of the utmost importance during these times. Are you always going to have that "NO." However, stay focused on the things of God.

God's will is to redeem you from the sins you have committed. If God "Called You," He knows who you are,

He will clean up your mess and bring you into your proper place.

"Release and take off the MASK!"
"Transformation is on the Rise!"

Notes to Myself

"Life has many wandering paths, stay the course until the end. It's your life.
-Mary V Pate

-12-
Great Faith

Faith walking, although I had done this so many times in my former life, it was so different when the time came to step out in ministry and moving in faith for God. Having "Great Faith" when you are sent to get people that you do not know is not an easy thing to do. It is a new mindset. But I knew that eventually I had to step out and be obedient to God. And so, I began my Great Faith Walk one day after the Holy Spirit yelled at me in His audible voice. That was not a good moment for me. He said, "You have got to have Great Faith." I trembled because of the sound.

'By faith [that is, with an inherent trust and enduring confidence in the power, wisdom, and goodness of God] we understand that the worlds (universe, ages) were framed and created [formed, put in order, and equipped for their intended purpose] by the word of God, so that what is seen was not made out of things which are visible." Hebrew 11:3

The evidence of things not seen are those things that are still in the spirit realm, but we cannot see or touch them.

Some may say that you should take a chance on executing new challenges, opportunities and you do not know the outcome. But this you do know is that God is faithful, and He is a rewarder of those who diligently seek Him.

One of the things we need to always realize is that when God wants us to do something for Him, whether it is ministry, Christian businesses, or mission trips, it is going to always take faith. In other words, God is saying "Are you going to do what I say? Are you going to go wherever I say go?" Whatever that thing is, it was for your benefit and the GLORY of God, because He showed up......AMEN!!!

What is God looking for In Us When He says, "Step out on Faith?" Stepping out on Faith for God is grabbing hold of your feelings and emotions, letting go of all the fear, moving out, and pressing towards the goal. YOU HAVE TO PUSH AND PRESS, PUSH AND PRESS.

He wants you to use the Authority and the Power that HE speaks of in:

> *"Behold I give you the Authority to trample on serpents and scorpions, and over all the power of the enemy, and nothing shall by any means hurt you."*
> *-Luke 10:19.*

He wants you to use your BOLDNESS and Confidence -

> *"Do not, therefore, fling away your [fearless] confidence, for it has a glorious and great reward. For you have need of patient endurance [to bear up under difficult circumstances without compromising], so that when you have carried out the will of God, you may receive and enjoy to the full what is promised."*
> ***-Hebrews 10:35-36***

The Faith Walk says, I am no longer standing still. I am going to do something, but I will stay in the "Will of God." You must be able to walk in the spirit, in God's will and God's way. Know that even when we slip; when we fall, we are only human. God will be right there to get us back on track. Gods got this. But before, we go out on our Faith Walk, we must believe and trust God and diligently seek him.

> *"But without faith it is impossible to [walk with God and] please Him, for whoever comes [near] to God must [necessarily] believe that God exists and that He rewards those who [earnestly and diligently] seek Him."*
> *- **Hebrews 11:6***

Let us not forget FEAR – there is always going to be some type of Fear that will show up when Faith is involved. Fear comes to contradict what FAITH is saying. Fear is the opposite of Faith. Fear's job is to stop you from doing what thus says the Lord. Fear's job is to stop you from reaching your God given destiny. Fear's job is to break you down. Fear's job is to steal your joy. Fear's job is to remove your name out of the Lamb's book. Bind and loose the neck of fear, like Jesus did the snake in the Garden of Gethsemane. Fear is the devil's work. Build your confidence and self-esteem. Encourage yourself to go after what God has for you. Your Faith Walk is your birth right from God.

Hebrews 11 gives us information and examples of those who stepped out on FAITH and completed the job God requested of them.

> *"By faith [with confidence in God and His word] Noah, being warned by God about events not yet seen, in reverence prepared an ark for the salvation of his family. By this [act of obedience] he condemned the world and became an heir of the righteousness which comes by faith."*
> **- Hebrews 11:7**

Noah being divinely warned of things not seen, moved with Godly fear (God's judgment). Fearing God is speaking of having a great sense of respect and submitting to Him. We should be aware that having respect for someone is doing right by them. So, we want to always do right by God. We should not want God to judge us because we're out of line or being disrespectful.

On the flip side "Can you imagine what Noah must have looked like, the gossip and rumors about him---40 years it took for the completion of the Ark. But, because Noah did what God requested and stepped out on **FAITH**; he saved his household, wife, children, other relatives, animals, by which he condemned the world and became heir of the righteousness which is according to **FAITH**.

Then there was Abraham. We can't forget that God told him to leave his home, his country and go out into a land that He would show him, and that He would make Abraham a great nation and bless him. *Genesis 12:1-20*. As you continue reading this story, you will see that Abraham took his cousin Lot with him, which eventually caused a problem. Here again, lets us know that everyone cannot travel with you. Be cognizant and understanding of that.

People of God – STEP out on FAITH. If God is telling you to do something, be sure that it is God. If you are not sure, ask Him – REPEAT – "FATHER – IS THIS YOUR VOICE I AM HEARING?" WAIT for a response. If no answer – DON'T MOVE. He will speak in His timing.

Remember, you will at times hear your own voice speaking in your ear. It is not so unusual for us to want or not want something so emphatically that we may hear ourselves speaking to ourselves. Let us not forget the voice of the enemy trying to stop you from moving forward. This is the reason for being certain as to which voice you hear. However, the more time you spend with the Holy Spirit will assure you of your ability to become familiar with His voice. Don't be shy or walking in unbelief and miss your opportunity to ask Him for instructions or to address your issues.

Ministry is not a "Call" giving you the go ahead to be like your friends. What God has for you ---is for YOU. What is it that God is speaking to you about, and are you afraid to step out on faith? Know this, God may have spoken to you years ago about a mission, but what is He speaking to you about NOW? Trust His NOW. What is it that the Holy Spirit is telling you to do? There is a perfect moment or time when God is telling you to "Move."

The only perfect time is when He is telling you to move. He is the only one who has perfect timing. Take the leap of faith, and just "MOVE." It may look strange to some, but to others, "It is just a move of God." Trust His NOW!

Be prepared to be talked about, persecuted and maybe a few eggs thrown at you, but trust me – you will survive it all. The Faith Walk is to benefit others; The Faith Walk is for God's Glory and The Faith Walk is for your Elevation and to show your obedience to God. Step out on faith. It is your life.

AMEN!!!!!!

-13-
Resting in God

What does it mean to "Rest in God?" God has a place for you when you may be tired or out of sync with Him or others. It's called "Resting in God." This simply means getting into his presence, and He will restore us. We become brand new in our Call to Order with Him, but this is the time to press on. Often, we try so intently to make things work in our lives, dealing with other people, and for some reason nothing seems to work out correctly. During those moments is when we need to stop, align ourselves with God, and press into Him. Allow the Holy Spirit to lead as it should be. Listen for His voice and allow Him to bring your mind at rest with Him.

Various people have different versions of God's Rest, but I am assured that the Rest and Peace we need to make it through every day is to give into the things of God. Respect and obey His commands, follow His instructions and He will direct your path. **Hebrews 3:16-19** gives a great analogy of Resting in God.

"For who were they who heard and yet provoked Him [with rebellious acts]? Was it

not all those who came out of Egypt led by Moses? And with whom was He angry for forty years? Was it not with those who sinned, whose dead bodies were scattered in the desert? And to whom did He swear [an oath] that they would not enter His rest, but to those who disobeyed [those who would not listen to His word]? So, we see that they were not able to enter [into His rest—the promised land] because of unbelief and an unwillingness to trust in God."
-Hebrews 3:16-19

It is so obvious in these scriptures that God is in control, and because of the disobedience of the people, they did not enter His rest. He was bringing them into His promised land, but because of their unbelief and unwillingness to trust God, they missed out on His great blessings.

I would say that whatever we need to do, the most important thing is to enter His Rest. Listen to His voice, obey His commands, and believe that His will is going to be done.

I would be remiss if I did not add these scriptures as an afterthought for you to ponder over regarding God's Rest. There are times when reading certain scriptures gives me a second boost of energy as I am perusing them, and revelations of how much God truly loves us is so very sincere. Join me in reading aloud **Hebrews 4:1-13 (Amplified Bible)**

The Believer's Rest

4 *"Therefore, while the promise of entering His rest still remains and is freely offered today, let us fear, in case any one of you may seem to come short of reaching it or think he has come too late. 2 For indeed we have had the good news [of salvation] preached to us, just as the Israelites also [when the good news of the promised land came to them]; but the message they heard did not benefit them, because it was not united with faith [in God] by those who heard. 3 For we who believe [that is, we who personally trust and confidently rely on God] enter that rest [so we have His inner peace now because we are confident in our salvation, and assured of His power], just as He has said,*

*"AS I SWORE [AN OATH]
IN MY WRATH, THEY SHALL
NOT ENTER MY REST,"*

[this He said] although His works were completed from the foundation of the world [waiting for all who would believe].

4 For somewhere [in Scripture] He has said this about the seventh day: "And God rested on the seventh day from all His works"; 5 and again in this, "They shall not enter My rest." 6 Therefore, since the promise remains for some to enter His rest, and those who formerly had the good news preached to them failed to [grasp it and did not] enter because of [their unbelief evidenced by] disobedience, 7 He again sets a definite day, [a new] "Today," [providing another opportunity to enter that rest by] saying through David after so long a time, just as has been said before [in the words already quoted],

"TODAY IF YOU HEAR HIS VOICE, DO NOT HARDEN YOUR HEARTS."

8 [This mention of a rest was not a reference to their entering into Canaan.] For if Joshua had given them rest, God would not speak about another day [of opportunity] after that. 9 So there remains a [full and complete] Sabbath rest for the people of God. 10 For the one who has once entered His rest has also rested from [the weariness and pain of] his [human] labors, just as God rested from [those labors uniquely] His own. 11 Let us therefore make every effort to enter that rest [of God, to know and experience it for ourselves], so that no one will fall by following the same example of disobedience [as those who died in the wilderness]. 12 For the word of God is living and active and full of power [making it operative, energizing, and effective]. It is sharper than any two-edged sword, penetrating as far as the division of the soul and spirit [the completeness of a person], and of both joints and marrow [the deepest parts of our nature], exposing and judging the very

thoughts and intentions of the heart. 13 And not a creature exists that is concealed from His sight, but all things are open and exposed, and revealed to the eyes of Him with whom we have to give account."
*-***Hebrews 4:1-13**

While reading these scriptures aloud, my Diversity Gifts of the Holy Spirit became alive within my soul. They make me want to bow down and admonish His Holy name for making me become so alive in my soul. And so, I have done just that.

Spiritual Gifts: Unity in Diversity

"There are diversities of gifts, but the same Sprit. There are differences of ministries, but the same Lord. And there are diversities of activities, but it is the same God who works all in all. But the manifestation of the Spirit is given to each one for the profit of all: for to one is given the word of wisdom through the Spirit, to another the word of knowledge through the same Spirit, to another faith by the same Spirit, to another gifts of healings by the same Spirit, to another the working of miracles, to another prophecy, to another discerning of spirits, to another different kinds of tongues, to another the interpretation of tongues.

But one and the same Spirit works all these things, distributing to each one individually as He wills."
                                          -1 Corinthians 12:1-11

    The Holy Spirit is His name. There are so many people who in this day are not aware of the many values of the Holy Spirit. Continue to walk in faith, read the word, and build the relationship you need to truly learn how the Holy Spirit can bless your life. I would not trade Him for nothing in the world and will preach His name across this nation.

    As the church would say, "Come on and Bless Him." Raise your hands, shout hallelujah, and bless His marvelous, His miraculous, His merciful, His loving and kind, His glorious and matchless name. Our *"Elohim (God) the majestic ruler over all."* We worship you.

Notes to Myself

-14-
Discerning the Voice of God

Too often I've encountered individuals who do not hear the voice of God. Often times, they may hear so many voices and can't distinguish between God's voice, their own voice, or the many other sounds we hear from day to day. I was speaking to a lady that said, "I have to be still sometimes to hear the voices." I asked, "What voices do you hear?" She responded, "Sometimes, two or three of them." I asked, "What do they say?" She responded, "Sometimes they tell me to do this, or to do that?" I discerned her frustration with me and backed off asking her questions. Then, I told her about a conversation I recently had with someone, and the person made a statement about me, and I knew the phrase did not originate from him, but from someone he had spoken to earlier. Immediately, the Holy Spirit spoke the name of the person in my ear who made the statement. Because I was on a mission for God, and those two persons tried to interfere and abolish my mission, the Holy Spirit immediately gave me the info I needed to make my next move, and so I did. My friend asked me "How do you know it was the Holy Spirit that spoke to you? I told her "I know the voice of God, and when I confronted the person, she did not deny her statement." Lord, Lord, Lord.

> *"And they heard the sound of the Lord God walking in the garden in the cool [afternoon breeze] of the day, so the man and his wife hid and kept themselves hidden from the presence of the Lord God among the trees of the garden."*
>
> -**Genesis 3:8**

As you can see, Adam and Eve heard the voice of God, but unfortunately, they eventually disobeyed Him. You see, God wants us to walk with Him. I say this all the time on social media, you will not hear the voice of the Lord without a relationship. Walking with Him, talking with Him, communing with Him, spending time with Him, reading His word. When we build a relationship with the Holy Spirit, He teaches you, increases your knowledge, gives you revelations, warns you about things, protects you from the enemy and so much more. I emphasize, "Always teaching you." You can't beat the Holy Spirit giving. Don't be religious on this subject, get real and become spiritual. The Holy Spirit is a spiritual being.

When you build a relationship with the Holy Spirit, you will become accustomed to His voice. His sudden words of knowledge He brings to you. Approximately a year ago, He brought me into His Silence, and while there, I became more and more aware of His ways. It is such an awesome thing to know that the person you are walking with can teach you so much, and you can't see Him. No one can do that accept through the Father, Son, and the Holy Spirit. I've been walking with the Holy Spirit for a very long time, and I would not exchange that for all the tea in China. This journey belongs to Him, and I accept the journey with grace. It's a true partnership.

People of God, it's time to rise. It's time to stop playing church, it's time to truly know who you serve. It's time to decipher one voice from another. The Holy Spirit is waiting on you to teach you all things.

Notes to Myself

-15-
Unlock Your Greatness

How do we get to the point of Unlocking Your Greatness?

Pick up your bootstraps and begin to move forward, without procrastinating, no fear, and looking beyond what is directly in front of you. You should not be moved by what you see, but instead looking beyond the barriers of things that try to hold you back. Whatever you see, God has planned that for you to see Him.

The word states:
"He who overcomes shall inherit all things, and I will be his God and he shall be My son."
- Rev. 21:7

Although we come against obstacles from time to time, there is no need to fear, but to go beyond what may be necessary for that time and season. Continue to push forward, and do not worry about what may happen, but instead put everything in the hands of the Holy Spirit and allow Him to move on your behalf. He wants to take care of you, in a way that only He can.

Be strong and of good courage. Move forward, you must build your courage and deal with the day-to-day stresses that may enter your life. Remember, no pain, no gain.

Although there may be obstacles, understand that if you do not make your life great, no one else is going to do it for you. Go ahead, Step into your Greatness and watch God work on your behalf. He is waiting on you to make the first step. Remember, God must see your Faith in action. Therefore, if you do not make a move, you will continue to stand still. Whatever you are after; you must want it very badly. Things may not work out the first time or the second time, but no matter what, keep on trying. Get up and start again. It is going to be OK. You have God's approval. He knows exactly who you are. He knows exactly where you are with your mission. Now, run with it.

Notes to Myself

-16-
A New Season

A new season in God is a new beginning. Don't mistake it, God does work in Seasons, and you will become a part of His seasons. As so many will say **"SHIFT."** Yes, there usually is a Shift in the atmosphere. I've come to know that the Holy Spirit's shifts or new seasons in my life come with new things, new ways to do things in my ministry, new missions, new things to learn and so much more. As the Holy Spirit said "He orchestrates my life" therefore; His timing to teach and elevate me to another level is exactly His Timing and Season. I'm just along to carry out His missions.

"There is a season (a time appointed) for everything and a time for every delight and event or purpose under heaven— A time to be born and a time to die; A time to plant and a time to uproot what is planted. A time to kill and a time to heal; A time to tear down and a time to build up. A time to weep and a time to laugh; A time to mourn and a time to dance. A time to throw away stones and a time to gather stones; A time to embrace and a time to refrain from embracing.

A time to search and a time to give up as lost; A time to keep and a time to throw away. A time to tear apart and a time to sew together; A time to keep silent and a time to speak. A time to love and a time to hate; A time for war and a time for peace.
Ecclesiastes 3:1-8

As you can see everything is about God's timing. I'm not saying it's an easy task to walk in God's timing; however, if you get out of line while He is directing your journey, He will pull you back in.

The information on the next page is a formality to give more understanding of the various structures of becoming licensed in ministry. Please know there may be differences in various states.

Notes to Myself

-17-

Licensed vs. Ordained

Licensed

Becoming licensed is a formality to give a person specific permission to do something. A preaching/ministry license gives permission to preach. Many organizations and churches give their ministers a license to preach. I have also heard in some cases if a minister leaves a church, he/she does not have permission to take that license with them. In other words, that license is only given by the authority of that specific church or organization and unfortunately, the rights of those people would be taken away if leaving that church. Some are saying that licenses are becoming obsolete. If a man or woman is *"Called"* to ministry, and that should only be according to the Call from God, why shouldn't they be allowed to speak freely? There are; however, some rules put into place that can hold a person back from moving forward in ministry or to keep them in place at their current home church.

Of course, there are countless denominations, religions and Christian ministries who have multiple rules regarding licensing and being ordained.

-18-
Ordained

To be ordained is putting a man/woman into position for the work of the ministry in whatever capacity God places them by the laying on of hands. This is what Paul told Timothy,

> *"Wherefore I put thee in remembrance that thou stir up the gift of God, which is in thee by the putting on of my hands."*
> *- 2 Timothy 1:6.*

Notice to stir up the gift of God. That could mean supernatural gifts, the diversities of gifts; however, the gifts point to having authority to exercise the workings of ministry for God Almighty. However, Paul saw the ordination of Timothy and the giving of gifts of God as necessary. This points to ordination as the giving of authority and potential that can be stirred up for the work of the Lord through the gifts no matter what they were.

> *Paul warned Timothy, "Do not hurry to lay hands on anyone [ordaining and approving someone for ministry or an office in the church, or in reinstating expelled offenders],*

and thereby share in the sins of others. keep yourself free from sin."
-1 Timothy 5:22.

Of course, this is particularly important even today. However, things have changed considerably across the board and considering the many ministry organizations depends on their beliefs as well.

Ordination permits the minister to perform church rites and sacraments, such as baptisms, legal marriages, and funerals. A judge, notary public, justice of the peace, and certain other public servants often officiate marriages as part of their job responsibilities. I recently witnessed a wedding being officiated by a family member and he was not in ministry. In all respects they are carrying out the same responsibilities for marriages as ordained ministers. Think about that. Two sets of rules.

As a follower of Christ, and knowing you are Called by God to be in ministry, walking in God's will and His ways, speaks volumes for who should or should not be ordained. However, some people live their lives for Jesus, and do not believe in being in ministry led by certain people. They have a right to choose who leads them in every facet of their lives. To know that you walk in God's will and His way should be the only reason to go forth in ministry. However, there are those who think you must have a leader (mankind) to lead you in ministry. Who took God out of the equation? Does God matter in this thinking process? Since God "Calls" God ordains. God does not make mistakes, and since He called you, He did not leave anything out of the matter. God still calls individuals that He "Called" for His specific purpose and reason. They are ordained by God. Again, He did not leave anything out of the equation. They are serving God and answering to God. No one should be stopped or hindered from doing ministry because they do not serve a woman or man in this process. Mankind should not call you into ministry without God having a Call on your life. The only true God I know is the Father, the Son, and the Holy Spirit. I have often seen statements from some leaders that a person is operating in a Jezebel spirit or walking in their own will if they do not have a woman or man as a leader. OK when we evaluate this, the question becomes "Who was the leader before you, and their leader their leader, and their leader, and so on and so forth? Stay with me on this because I am going somewhere. We can go back 200-300 years and find that preachers got a Call from God, stepped out and began to do God's will. There was no one before them except God. More than likely in most places there was no other preachers around perhaps for miles, states, etc. Harriet Tubman did not have anyone except the Holy Spirit to tell her all that she knew. There was no mankind around to lead her. The Holy Spirit led her, and she brought many people out of slavery. Let us be truthful, every day we see ministry leaders falling, others living ungodly lives behind closed doors and more. It behooves all of us to seek God seriously before you choose a leader. We choose government officials, choose your leader in ministry if you so wish. It is your choice. When you hear the Call, it is coming from God, and there will be many things you will go through while coming into ministry at times. Refer to the previous chapters and seek God for all you do before Him. Believe me, the Holy Spirit can and will give you all the answers you need for your ministry Call. Not everyone is the same. God **Called** in biblical times, anointed in biblical times, appointed in biblical times, and whatever He did not do, He sent someone else to do it for Him. He is still doing that today. Reading the Word has the answers.

Your Life has been Predestined!

Notes to Myself

-19-
The Called

And so, you are one of the Called. Take some time and look back before you knew you had a Call on your life. No matter how long it takes you to walk into your Call, that Call awaits you stepping into it.

Having a *"Call"* on your life is one of the best things you will ever experience once you accept and surrender to the Call. I believe everyone has a Call on their lives; however, the real test is whether you will accept and embrace that Call. A Call can be more than a Ministry Call; however, the Call is there. Calls on our lives exist when people have a dire need to exercise specific tasks in their communities, becoming president of the United States, State Representatives, the burden to find criminals, and so many more areas we can call out. When these burdens come into your life, they become passions you need to fulfill. I would say, "That person is Called to do the work and will not stop until it is done." We have all watched movies that involved someone finding a killer; as such, and would spend years searching for that person, never giving up. That is because they had a strong burden to find that killer and would stop at nothing to get the job done. I call that having a Call on their life to finish the work.

However, I have often wondered what a person's life is like if they never accept the Call. I can only imagine that there must be uneasy feelings of anxiety, frustration, and burdens in their stomachs. Feelings that there is always something missing. The problem may be that so many people do not take the time or have the originality to seek their calling. And because of the lack to find that originality often people just exist from day to day. I believe the most important reason some people do not accept their Call is because they do not want their lives to be transformed. Once you accept the Call, you will realize there was nothing so important in your past life to return to. It does not matter who God called you to be, how you were called, and what you went through while walking in your Call, He saved you through it all for such a time as this.

One of the disturbing things I have found is that some people do not know their calling. Instead of waiting for mankind to give you an answer, seek God first. As I was coming into ministry, there were times when I was given an incorrect title by man; however, God never leaves us without answers. All we need to do is ask the questions. Secondly, do not try and be like someone else. Remove the spirit or desire to be and act like another person. What God has for you is for you.

Believe that God has a Purpose and Plan for all of us. When the *"Call"* comes, "Answer the Call-You have been Chosen for." Your Life was Predestined. Walk it Out!

> *"And those whom He predestined, He also called; and those whom He called, He also justified [declared free of the guilt of sin]; and those whom He justified, He also glorified [raising them to a heavenly dignity]."*
> ***- Romans 8:30***

Notes to Myself

-20-
Conclusion

Years ago, the Holy Spirit awakened me early hours of the morning on two occasions and had me to say this: **First:** He said, "Open your mouth and say this, as I opened my mouth these words came forth "I am an Apostle". **Second:** "Open your mouth and say this, and the words came forth "I am a Messenger." Realizing I did not say the words specifically although they came through me, it was The Holy Spirit who spoke the words through me. It was my first practice in learning to hear and say those words myself. One thing we can be sure of is that the Holy Spirit can and will teach you all things, you only need to be open to receive. I surely did not know who I was in ministry at that time, but I asked Him. In His Timing, He gave me the answers through me. I did not want this once I learned what these titles meant. I begged, cried, and screamed for Him to take them back. However, he did not listen to me, but only began to have me walk into this ministry with a quickness.

The Holy Spirit brought me into ministry as Paul was by Jesus in **2 Corinthians 1:1-2** *"Paul, an apostle of Jesus Christ by the will of God, and Timothy our brother, To the church of God which is at Corinth, with all the* *saints who are in all Achaia Grace to you and peace from God our Father and the Lord Jesus Christ."*

As the Holy Spirit was bringing me into ministry, He said "I orchestrate your life." And so, He does.

Notes to Myself

Contact Info

Public Speaking Engagements:
Email: mpateministries@gmail.com

Ministry:
https://maryvpate.com

Public Speaking:
Mary's books are on:
https://maryvpate.com

Books by Mary V. Pate

- **"8 Golden Rules -** How to Move Yourself Out of the Way"
- ***"10 Powerful Keys***: *Letting Go - Living a Victorious Life"*
- **"Now I Have the Best Job** in the World – How God Helped Me Through Sabotage in the Workplace"

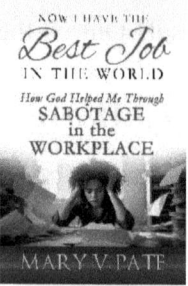

I give all the Glory to God!

Mary Pate constantly seeks after the heart of God, walks in an apostolic ministry led by the Holy Spirit, and went through His wilderness school of long suffering for many years. He has launched her out into ministry focused on leading women's conferences, and workshops teaching the word of God on diverse topics that were led by the Holy Spirit, with instructions on how to apply the word of God directly to your life. The Lord has led Mary into a healing and deliverance ministry of mind, body, and spirit. She is an Apostle, Author, Certified Transformational Life Coach, Inspirational Speaker, Conference Leader, and Kingdom Trainer. As a Called Writer, she has written several books orchestrated by the Holy Spirit to reach the masses and continues to write words brought forth by Him. ***Now I have the Best Job in the World and*** became an Amazon Best Seller.

Mary's journey while coming into Ministry was arduous to say the least, losing everything, broke, busted and disgusted on many occasions. She said, "Suffering would be an under-statement, but she continues to move forward by the teachings of the Holy Spirit.

Mary Pate's Ministries is committed to teaching others how to live victorious and successful lifestyles. She states, "I was born to walk in my *"Call – Chosen by God."*

Advancing the Kingdom

www.ingramcontent.com/pod-product-compliance
Lightning Source LLC
Chambersburg PA
CBHW070306100426
42743CB00011B/2372